W9-BIC-150

ZEN

ROCK
GARDENING

ZEN

ROCK
GARDENING

by Abd al-Hayy Moore

RUNNING PRESS
PHILADELPHIA · LONDON

Copyright © 1992 by Running Press.

All rights reserved under the Pan-American and International
Copyright Conventions.

The poems "Poem on Dry Mountain" and "All Worries and Troubles" by Muso Soseki, translated by W.S. Merwin and Sōiku
Shigematsu, are reprinted by permission from *Sun at Midnight:
Poems and Sermons by Muso Soseki* by North Point Press, Transla-
tion copyright © 1989 by W.S. Merwin and Sōiku Shigematsu.

*This book may not be reproduced in whole or in part in any form
or by any means, electronic or mechanical, including photocopying,
recording, or by any information storage and retrieval system now
known or hereafter invented, without written permission from the
publisher.*

12 13 14 15

Digit on the right indicates the number of this printing.

Library of Congress Cataloging-in-Publication Number 92-53680

ISBN 1-56138-148-9 (package)

Edited by Melissa Stein
Interior design by Jacqueline Spadaro
Picture research by Gillian Speeth
Cover design by Toby Schmidt
Cover photo © Tony Stone Worldwide
Line drawings by Helen Driggs
Typography: ITC Garamond with CG Omega, by COMMCOR,
    Philadelphia, Pennsylvania
Printed in The United States

This book may be ordered by mail from the publisher. Please add
$2.50 for postage and handling. *But try your bookstore first!*

Running Press Book Publishers
125 South Twenty-second Street
Philadelphia, Pennsylvania 19103-4399

To the memory of my Zen teacher,
Master Shunryu Suzuki, 1905–1971

CONTENTS

OPENING THE GATE

The perfection of Zen is to be perfectly and simply human.

Alan Watts (1915–1973)
English scholar and writer

To see a world in a grain of sand,

And a heaven in a wild flower,

Hold infinity in the palm of your hand,

And eternity in an hour.

William Blake (1757–1827)
English poet

Entering a garden is like opening

a book. You step in, look around,

recognize some of the garden's

unique characteristics. There may

be clear paths, formal patterns of

growth cleanly clipped, greenery or

sentences shaped just so, or your

impression may be of wild nature

left more or less on its own. You may

be happily drawn in by the garden's

peacefulness, its slopes and flower-

ings, or be deeply

excited by its strange-

ness. It may bring a

stillness to your

nerves, let your mind

float, sweeten your soul, or, like a

book, reach down into some darker

earthiness of your more secret

nature. Gardens have a power

 hidden in their

leaves and

stones.

A garden frames certain ele-

ments in nature which might

otherwise be overlooked. It empha-

sizes certain plants or rocks by

careful choice and arrangement,

and draws bold contrasts between

rough and smooth, delicate and

tough. When you read further into

a book, a novel perhaps, you may

meet characters that are rough or

smooth, delicate or tough. Or in a

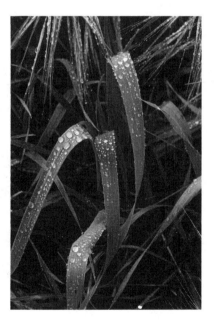

garden, as in a book, surrounded

with unfamiliar scenery and new

things to look at, it may be yourself you meet.

In a book, which surrounds us with its own frames of reality, fiction or nonfiction, nothing is real. When we read, we allow ourselves, even openly court, the luxury of being deceived by an illusion, in

hopes of gaining knowledge, relaxation, or pleasure. In the same way,

there is reality as well as unreality
about a garden. It has been cultivated intentionally,
has a beginning and
end, an entrance
and an exit, has
been set up for a
reason, and can put
us in an unac-
customed frame of
mind, guiding us to see things in a
new way.

Both garden and book take us on
their paths. A garden leads us to its
central plot: a wider view—the
unhurried contemplation of earth's
beauties, often hidden from sight.
We find ourselves slowing down,

Chinese

calligraphy,

meaning ''Zen.''

surrounded now by growing things,

looking at a flowering bush in the

time it takes to read a sentence or

a paragraph instead of just passing

by. We see our own natures against

the background of earth's organic

time-flow instead of our usual

social time-flow of hurry and frus-

tration. Then we have the sense that

we are not merely observers mean-

dering along pointlessly, but

essential observers focusing on fresh observations. And we may become, for a moment, perfect empty observers.

That is when what is small takes on a bigger resonance, when we have the chance to glimpse the meaning of the world in a grain of sand, for it has been framed in a majestic simplicity. In a garden we may open our minds in the face of nature, stilling our preconceptions, and opening up the possibility of viewing our selves and our usual ways of thinking from an entirely different perspective. A true breath of fresh air may blow through us.

We now understand that the act

of removing a rectangular wooden

frame, a little plastic bag of sand

and stones, and a

miniature wooden

rake from a card-

board box can be

the beginning of a lifelong adven-

ture of seeing things in a new way.

This garden may enable you to enter

into a tradition that goes as far back

as 3000 B.C., and is as near to you in

time as your next breath, your next

thought, or your next perception.

GARDENS OF THE MIND

Heaven and earth and I are of the same root,
The ten-thousand things and I are of one substance.

Zen Master Sojo (384–414 A.D.)

The Japanese for centuries have cultivated all kinds of gardens, delicate and picturesque, cool and relaxing, powerful and dramatic. The islands of Japan, filled with lush greenery—flowering plants such as azaleas and chrysanthemums, and massive cedar and fir trees—are veritable gardens in

themselves, apart from the overcrowded modern cities.

A strong love and even venera-
tion of nature has led to an
aesthetic of natural beauty that
appears characteristic of the entire
culture. The Japanese are known for
their annual expeditions to view
spring's first cherry blossoms, as
well as for a love of miniaturized
trees (*bonsai*) and flower arranging

(*ikebana*). The
Japanese term
for tranquility,
aesthetics, and
"viewing" (as in
viewing something beautiful), is
Yugen, which also has the meaning
of "bringing about inner harmony."
The great Zen scholar D. T.

Suzuki theorized that this innate

love of nature may have much to do

Japan's Mt. Fuji
inspires awe and
peacefulness.

with the central presence of Mt.

Fuji, seen as a mixture of beauty,

awesomeness, and majestic

austerity, on the main island of

Japan. An extinct volcano, Mt. Fuji

was once capable of wreaking

destruction on the land and its peo-

ple. Yet the great woodblock artist,

Hokusai (1760–1849), made hun-

dreds of pictures of Fuji at various

seasons and from various angles. In

one print this once-furious moun-

tain is viewed through a spider's

web! It is clear that something in

the Japanese soul loves to isolate

basic elements in nature in order to

bring about psychological repose

and intellectual calm. Even spiritual

enlightenment!

The Zen rock garden is an

example of this setting off and

framing. Here we encounter the

totally unexpected, for which no

previous garden experience has

adequately prepared us. Even the

word "garden" may not be an

appropriate term for these almost

otherworldly creations. They do not

fit into any of our own cultural

contexts, and may confront our

expectations much like modern art

installations where an artist places

21

on the museum floor a mass with a
hard-to-identify shape, formed from
unknown materials.

A Different Garden

We usually find Zen rock gardens
in areas between buildings of Zen
monasteries, in inner courtyards, or
in areas adjacent to normally land-
scaped gardens. Familiar paths and
vegetation are replaced by a stark
rectangle of flat raked gravel,
grouped or single stones, and
space. The gravel is usually white or
gray, combed in long, perfectly
straight rows, wavy patterns, scal-
lops, or concentric circles around
the rocks. The rocks are various

shades of dark gray, black, even

greenish-black, and stand up from

the flat surface—imposingly

austere, streaked, flinty, and immov-

able in the silent space. Space, and

more space, with a breath of the

infinite in it. Space that extends all

the way out from these solemn

stones to the sun and stars.

The immediate impression of a

Zen rock garden is both soothing

and shocking. To come upon one of

these gardens in ordinary life is to

seem to break through the veiled

appearances of material reality into

a sudden stillness, almost deathly

stillness, of a more essential reality.

Like *The Wizard of Oz* in reverse,

out of the Technicolor of our day-to-day lives we are suddenly transported into a garden of black and white.

This is the Zen rock garden, called *kare-sansui* (withered land-scapes) in Japanese. These gardens

Evenly combed sand patterns in Ryoan-ji garden, Kyoto

cannot be entered in the usual sense, but are meant to be *viewed*.

Embodying the Zen Buddhist desire

to turn away from the life of this

world in order to find our true and

essential natures,

Zen rock gardens

both disarm and

empower us. They

are so radically

different from all other gardens we

have known that our usual responses

must give way to deeper ones.

The rock gardens' resonant,

austere appearance echoes an

intense spiritual striving, and

indeed many of these rock gardens

are places for the prolonged and

rigorous practice of Zen meditation,

some even providing flat-topped

Chinese

calligraphy,

meaning

''Flowing water.''

rocks on which to meditate.

Emptied of the usual garden

elements such as plants and trees,

Zen rock gardens serve as perfect

backdrops to empty ourselves

of our own frivolous clutter,

our clung-to experiences and

passionately-held views, to get

down to basics and see things in a
new way.

The gardens are a means to dis-
cover the sources and strengths of
our natural humanity, which,

according to Zen teaching, is
poised, calm, sincere, and capable
of facing all matters in life with
equanimity and perfect composure.
The contemplative experience in
Zen is meant to awaken the primal
consciousness hidden within us
which makes possible any spiritual
activity, big or small.

In this poem,
a Zen master
encourages his
student with
seemingly
nonsensical
anecdotes.

Zen rock gardens seem at once

both remote and intimate. They

have been called "mental gardens"

or "gardens of the mind." They par-

take of the crisp, clear mental

realizations associated with Zen

teaching, when the world for a

moment is turned upside-down and

in one flash an illuminated view unravels life's conundrums. These awakenings often lead to laughter— liberating ripples of laughter like gurgling mountain streams.

It is the sudden, stark monochrome of these rock gardens that may jog the mind into Big Mind, the Universal Mind, of Zen.

The Universal Mind

The clean, crisp elements of Zen rock gardens mirror the experience of mind with a capital "M"—meaning not our usual dreary mental chatter, but the natural part of our consciousness that connects us to the Universal Mind, the living

consciousness of the whole of creation. This understanding of mind is, to Zen practitioners, the original human state, not only in the sense of ourselves as children first experiencing the world with immediacy, spontaneity, and delight, but also in the sense of humankind's soulful, original openness on earth, the simple condition of being human.

Zen masters talk not only about enlightenment, but about re-enlightenment—not about striving laboriously for something we haven't got and have to achieve, but rather about entering into the living experience of an enlightenment that is already ours by our very nature. It is a matter of rediscovering natal territory that was ours before our own personal creation— what Zen teachers often call "our original face." This is a realm of the spirit that is more intense, but also calmer, slower, and more contemplative than the state of mind in which we are used to conducting our lives.

In Zen rock gardens this slowness seems almost to decelerate to absolute zero. Nothing grows, except a bit of moss on the bases of the rocks, and in some rock gardens even all traces of moss are carefully

removed. But, as in the slowness of
Gregorian chant, which in some
ways resembles the chanting performed in Buddhist monasteries,
this simplification of elements
sacrifices mental
excitement in order
to amplify subtle
details often overlooked.

The experience of our little
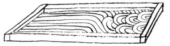 wooden-frame
rock garden with
its sand and small stones may not
be quite the same as the experience
we might have in a
full-sized rock gar-
den, but we may
nevertheless understand. We may

see that behind this miniature garden of ours lie centuries of disciplined striving and spiritual development. Remembering that the Big Bang theory of the origin of the universe puts forth the idea that all matter was first condensed into something about the size of a grain of sand, we may go from our miniature rock garden *bang* into a new way of seeing. Even with this replica

rock garden, with living space all
around us, we may yet touch our
elemental core, and at the same
time realize the wider view.

*Sand cone and
raked gravel in
the garden of
Ginkaku–ji,
Kyoto*

GARDENS OF PARADISE

We might imagine that a history
of gardens would be shrouded in
pure speculation, especially
gardens that were established as
early as the 8th century. But

Chinese and Japanese historical chronicles record the creation and development of many gardens, especially those connected to ritual centers, royal compounds, temples, or parks owned or frequented by nobles

Japanese calligraphy, meaning "Japanese landscape gardening."

of the court. Often, the names of their designers—architects and expert gardeners—were preserved.

Every culture creates artifacts in this world that represent a collective vision of the next or invisible world—such as Egyptian deities and tomb paintings, or Mexican temples and statuary. Thus it is not surpris-

ing that the earliest gardens of the

Chinese, the people with the oldest

continuous recorded history on

earth, were representations of their

belief in a perfect paradise.

Taoism: A Name for
What Cannot Be Named

We seek it but cannot see it;
    we call it "subtle."
We listen to it but cannot hear it;
    we call it "essential."
We reach for it but cannot grasp it;
    we call it "serene."

        Lao-tzu (6th century B.C.?)
        Chinese philosopher

Taoism, a philosophy and cos-

mology articulated in all its

paradoxical ambiguity by Lao-tzu in

the *Tao Te Ching,* actually dates

back to 3000 B.C., with the gradual

compilation of the *I Ching,* a book

of oracles used in divination.

Taoism is a way of seeking to

become one with the eternal fluctu-

ations in nature, flowing with those

changes through a kind of positive

non-action. An ancient vision

described a pure and transcendent

Land of the Immortals, which

adepts at Taoist practices longed to

enter. Based on these beliefs,

emperors and nobles created

gardens that resembled this para-

dise, with lacy pavilions floating on

water as if on clouds, replicas of

celestial pleasure boats on celestial

lakes, and places of eternal calm

and luxury. Their gardens contained rocks that stood for the sacred mountains where the Immortals dwelt—heavenly landscapes viewed across stretches of water, casting evanescent reflections on their rippling surfaces.

A Taoist landscape architect would study the individual rocks he planned to use in order to best combine them by virtue of their "dragon-veins" (*feng-shui* in Chinese), invisible deep energies thought to run between all objects in the material world. The resulting gardens seem alive, with majestic rocks occupying places of honor, almost conversing among them-

selves. Visitors today sense living

energies in the finest of these

ancient gardens without knowing

anything of their underlying occult

cosmology.

Classical Chinese painting often

portrayed human beings as specks

in a huge landscape, and Chinese

gardens imitated, in miniature, the

eft and right:

Ming Dynasty

croll paintings

y Chinese artist

Dong Quichang

epict the

astness of

ature.

awesome mountain wilds of the

Chinese countryside, with towering

peaks and deep, craggy canyons.

Painting masters often created deli-

cate but overpowering scenes of

great mountains, sheer cliffs, silvery

waterfalls, ghost-like rocks grimac-

ing and hovering, and then added a

tiny, ragged hermit sitting in front of his wind-blown hut, his face beaming upward at the moon, so surrounded by pure awesomeness as to have one foot in heaven—or at least his head in the clouds. One famous 5th-century Taoist painter wrote, "Landscapes have a material existence, and yet reach into a spiritual domain."

Rocks in Transit

China was the trend-setter in Japan's early eras. Ideas about painting and gardens migrated from China to Japan and were eagerly emulated by native students. Often these ideas mingled with ancient beliefs already being practiced. Receptive to the Taoist appreciation of rocks, Japanese believers in spirits had already been making meaningful arrangements of rocks both as altars to their gods and as actual manifestations of those divine beings from before the 5th century A.D., the beginning of Japan's recorded history.

Shinto, the pre-Buddhist creed native to Japanese soil, celebrated numerous rituals to spirits (*kami*) believed to inhabit all natural phenomena, including plants, storms, and even whistling echoes through mysterious gorges. The sacred ground in Shinto shrines was

Rocks linked by ropes mark off sacred ground i Ise Bay near Futami, Japan.

often marked off with stones, or stones connected by loosely hanging ropes, and the temple grounds themselves were covered with layers of pebbles, forerunner of the surface gravel of Zen rock gardens.

Buddhism entered Japan in the 6th century and brought with it a highly idealized cosmology that was later mirrored in luxurious garden designs, influenced in part by the paradisical Taoist visions of China. Central to many of these gardens was an imposing mound of earth in imitation of Mount Shumisen, an ideal mountain sacred to Buddhists as the exalted residence of many venerable Buddhas. In all of these gardens, artistic arrangements of

Sand cones at Kamigato shrine, Kyoto represent idealized Buddhist mountains.

rocks were used symbolically to spur the religious imagination into thinking of holy beings, holy dwelling-places, holy mountains, holy moments. This symbolic presence would achieve the height of purified abstraction in the Zen rock gardens to come.

WARRIORS AND MONKS

Sitting quietly, doing nothing.
Spring comes, and the grass grows by itself.

Zen poem

Based solidly on the tenets of Buddha's teachings, Zen, the "mystical" branch of Buddhism, was established in Japan in 1191. The Buddha taught spiritual detachment and supreme enlightenment as the way to be released from the implacable wheel of birth, suffering, and death that rotates through all our lives, and he encouraged his disciples to help others gain release as well.

As in all the mystical branches of the major religions, such as the Christian mystics, the Hasidim, and the Sufis, Zen practitioners desire to experience enlightenment firsthand. Followers are willing to make sacrifices and undergo necessary disciplines, rather than merely honor the teacher or the teachings through external, formalized rituals. In this way sects such as Zen might actually be called practical rather than mystical, since they take the deepest truths of their teachings seriously and attempt to put them directly into practice.

During the 12th century in Japan, samurai warriors, freed from service to their noble masters, gradually replaced the nobles in power in society. They were attracted to Zen as a form of Buddhism that was stripped to its barest essentials, spartan and vigorous in its practices, upholding warrior virtues of honor and correct behavior.

More and more samurai became monks and priests, in hopes of achieving direct insight into their own natures (*satori*), as the reward for their strenuous efforts of self-control. Those who entered the path of Zen also hoped to realize the irreversible illumination of Nirvana, a state of ineffable peace, free from the world of space and time, free from the rotating wheel. Zen's no-nonsense approach, full of hard work, paradoxes, and sudden realizations,

In the Brooklyn Botanic Garden's Japanese Garden. Clockwise from far left: Snow-view Lantern; Kasuga stone lantern; Torii, or "gateway to heaven," indicating the presence of a shrine.

appealed to the samurai taste, and
was also suited to the warrior
temperament.

Zen teaching trained monks in
endurance, rugged service, and self-
effacement, but at the core of the
spiritual flowering was an emphasis
on sincerity, enabling one to see
swiftly into the heart of a matter

with unhesitating directness and
humanity. This new outlook
brought about a change in aes-

*Chinese
calligraphy,
meaning "life
energy."*

thetics as well, and the courtly,
effete beauty of art, architecture,
and gardens gave way to the appreciation of an almost primordial,
elemental starkness, expressing the
"sincerity" of Zen teaching.

Father of the Rock Garden

Muso Soseki, a Zen priest and poet known as the father of the Zen rock garden, was born on the western coast of Japan in 1275 (ten years after the birth of Dante in Florence), and died in 1351 in a temple on the outskirts of Kyoto, where he had created one of his last rock gardens.

Already a renowned and venerated Zen priest in his mid-sixties, Muso was called upon to design gardens on the grounds of numerous Zen monasteries, making use of rocks as settings for real spiritual enlightenment in the midst of nature. He made masterful use of

the natural terrain, and often

placed rocks in such a way that they

seemed to have been there for

millenia, pushing their craggy bulks

out of the womb of the ground.

Muso's garden in western Kyoto,

called Saiho-ji, contains a combina-

tion of solid, dark rocks with

brooding shapes overshadowed by

tempest-gnarled trees. A visitor to

this garden feels surrounded by the

protective reality of the natural ele-

ments and, at the same time,

isolated in a remote, slightly savage

place near the raw rock-heart of the

earth. In other gardens, Muso

created a kind of spiritual optical

illusion, setting up streaked, light-

colored vertical rocks to look like

waterfalls, and spreading white gravel at the bases of these "water-falls" to resemble pools.

In the tradition of Zen masters, Muso wrote many poems express-ing the varieties of Zen experience, some specifically connected to his rock gardens, such as the *Poem on Dry Mountain (A Zen Garden):*

> *A high mountain*
> *soars without*
> *a grain of dust*
> *a waterfall*
> *plunges without*
> *a drop of water*
> *Once or twice*
> *on an evening of moonlight*
> *in the wind*
> *this man here*
> *has been happy*
> *playing the game that suited him*

Many of Muso's gardens were

landscapes of immensity realized in

miniature, the awesome forces of

nature reduced to a human scale a

Zen meditator could cope with. This

is in keeping with the practice of

Zen, which is to overcome the world

as an opposing force and become

one with it as an ever-moving, ever-

changing positive force. This is

achieved by concentrating on natural breathing rhythms in a formal posture of meditation.

Traditionally, new students of Zen are cautioned against meditating too close to the open sea, since the passion of the tumultuous ocean is so overpowering that it may be too difficult to quiet one's inner being. Better to sit in meditation next to a stream, where its gentle energies can become more peacefully assimilated. And perhaps even better is to sit in a garden of stones *resembling* islands surrounded by etched gravel *resembling* the sea, to find that still point, that unwobbling pivot from which any obstacle

Haboku, or "flung-ink" landscape. Hanging scroll by the Japanese artist Shugetsu, Muromachi period.

may be confronted from a position of unflappable strength.

Brush-strokes and Rock Patterns

An uncanny thing happened in the development of the Zen rock garden, unprecedented in the history of gardens. Rather than pictorial art recording the way gardens looked, as in Indian miniatures or the paintings of the French Impressionists, in Japanese cultural history the actual design of gardens was influenced by two-dimensional ink paintings.

Well-trained Zen monks were

often able to express their experiences of Zen in various mediums (besides hard work around the monastery), including calligraphy, poetry, gardening, and *sumi-e* ink painting. *Sumi-e* ink paintings are created with soft brushes and black ink (charcoal mixed with sizing and water) used almost straight from the pot or thinned to transparent grays. They are entirely monochromatic, going from dense, velvety black to faint wisps of gray.

The resulting paintings are like flashes of insight—a perfect few lines and washes portraying a tall cliff in the mist with a few pines and

a skiff on the lake at its base, a bowl

of plums, or a cat stretching out by

some bent bamboo—marvelous in

their ability to say so much with so

little. To be in the presence of some

of these paintings is much like hear-

ing the loud shouts Zen masters use

to wake up the sleeping spirit of a

student who is teetering on the

brink of realization.

Many of the best Japanese ink painters were also designers of gardens, such as Sesshu Toyo of the 15th century, master artist of all Japan in his time. At least four gardens attributed to Sesshu are still in existence, including the Mampuku-ji and Iko-ji gardens in Shimane Prefecture, and the garden of Joei-ji temple, near Yamaguchi.

Imitation of grandiose natural scenes (such as mountain peaks) in extremely reduced proportions, already a common element in garden design, was filtered further through the imaginative visions of such deft and suggestive ink paintings as Sesshu's. The result was the

rock gardens as we now know them,
compositions in shades of black
and gray and blinding white (gravel
equalling the blank white spaces
left unpainted on the rice
paper or silk of the
scrolls), the textures of
the stones and gravel
often "feathering off" the
same way ink strokes fade
into the background of a
painting.

In the early 1600s, about the time
of the birth of the English poet Mil-
ton, a Chinese how-to book on
painting called *The Mustard-Seed
Garden Painting Manual* was
introduced into Japan. Among its

subjects (vegetation, trees, mountains, and human figures) are 16
techniques for painting groups of
rocks, and arranging rocks into
pleasing compositions. Examples of
rock groupings from *The Mustard-
Seed Garden Painting Manual* were
imitated in the rock gardens dating
from this period.

The transformation from ink
painting to rock garden, one imitated view of reality influencing
another, connects us to the miniature rock garden. Our experience
with a wooden frame, sand, stones,
and rake might be looked upon as
an exercise in symbolism, in crea-
tive imagining, in seeing one thing

standing for another. Full-scale rock gardens have an impact different from these miniature ones on our office desks or tables at home, but the effect of our involvement with them may also be to give us aesthetic distance, to detach ourselves with sublime equanimity from the knotty entanglements of our daily lives.

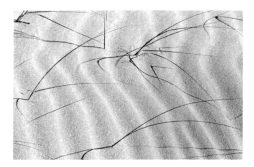

In Zen, we want to do everything with presence of mind. It is in a grain of sand that we may see the world, not in some generalized

notion or abstract idea of "sand."

The detachment of Zen is not a

blank haze of abstraction, but a

state in which we still pay attention

to particulars—even closer atten-

tion than usual.

ROCKS AND SAND

Driven by the compulsion to make the invisible,
mysterious forces of nature and space tangible, man
saw one particular substance stand out in the gloom
of primeval nature—solid, immovable rock.

> Kenzo Tange
> 20th-century Japanese landscape archite

Rocks, rocks, rocks, and more

rocks! Big rocks, little rocks, rocks

that look like mountains, rocks at

our feet that rattle when we walk

down a mountain trail, huge rocks in rivers that stick up like surprised bears out of the rushing water. Rocks in our heads!

The choice of rocks is crucial in creating full-scale Zen rock gardens. Japan has rock nurseries as elaborate as any Western country's plant nurseries, and some of the most remarkable rocks may cost as much as $10,000 each.

Since their role in a rock garden is to evoke something else, the most highly prized rocks have suggestive

shapes and sizes. A prospective

garden de-

signer might

look for rocks

that resemble

mountains

glimpsed from afar, islands with

mountains, tall waterfalls with cas-

cades falling

straight down

to their bases,

living things like turtles, cranes,

tigers, oysters, and hares, which

have folkloric references—and,

of course,

Buddhas.

Rocks, once

chosen, are not simply placed on

the surface, but buried two-thirds

into the ground, to appear as

Tofuku-ji temple

in Kyoto, with

sand combed in

swirls like

cascading water

natural outcrops. The direction of

the rocks' edges and ridges, and

their overall placement in relation

to each other, are carefully consi-

dered to allow the free expression

of their natural energy, taking into

Veranda and rocks at Ryoan-ji, Kyoto

account the Taoist mystery of "dragon-veins." There are never any traces of mortar or concrete, and never any refinements that show the human touch, such as polishing with oil or adding color. The natural patina of weathering is prized above all else.

Rocks of Many Faces

Rocks are classified in numerous

ways, usually in categories of five.

One category classifies them

according to place of origin: Moun-

tain rocks, valley rocks, river rocks,

marine rocks, and water stones, the

last taken from river beds, like the

ones in our miniature garden.

Another category classifies them
according to basic shapes: Master
rocks, upright and dignified,
representing stability; pillar rocks,
tall and tree-like; branch rocks,

jagged and lateral, corresponding

to the snapping zig-zags of fire;

base stones, resembling calm lakes

or flat bodies of water; and root
stones, corresponding to the earth,
but also resembling a windswept
shore or rush of rapids.

The most subtle and sophisti-

Chines

calligraphy

meaning ''Tao.''

cated classification is based upon

five types of symbolism: natural,

mood, idea, spiritual, and melodic.

Natural symbolism includes the

resemblance of rock shapes to

other elements in nature, such as

waterfalls and mountains. In mood

symbolism rocks personify human characteristics such as nobility, heroism, or even eccentric wit.

Idea symbolism is more complex, referring to stories or images which require previous knowledge on the part of the beholder. One especially vivid example of idea symbolism is a small garden at Ryogen-in, designed in the 15th century. The image depicts a drop of water that has just fallen into a vast sea, made from a flat dark stone in the center of a series of concentric circles etched in gray gravel. One can almost hear the "plop"—even in the gravel! The image suggests that Buddha's teaching is a vast sea, and

when a drop of rain falls into it
(symbolizing in turn the human
seeker), a large ripple is created,
causing untold reverberations, circle upon circle of ripples echoing
out to an unforeseeable edge.

Spiritual symbolism is
suggested when the
energy of movement in an
arrangement of rocks is
like the feeling we get
from the swiftness and
grace of written calligraphy. Stones may seem to

pursue or flee each other, or the
rocks may have their "backs"
turned to each other, as in a lovers'
quarrel.

Finally, melodic symbolism occurs when the shapes of rocks and their arrangements in relation to each other resemble the highs and lows, the louds and softs, of sound—in Ryoan-ji, one of the most famous of Japan's rock gardens from the 15th century, commentators have noted that there is an element of melodic call and response between the ·five groups of rocks, like the chanting of Buddhist scriptures heard at dawn in Zen monasteries.

The Garden of Ryoan-ji

The rock garden of Ryoan-ji in Kyoto is perhaps the apotheosis of

the art. For five centuries, people

have made pilgrimages to visit this

garden, spending hours or even

days on its long veranda benches,

View of the

northeast corner

of Ryoan-ji,

Kyoto

nourished by its visionary possibili-

ties, puzzled by its meanings.

Built in 1488, Ryoan-ji is part of a

monastery, and covers an area

about the size of a tennis court. A

wide veranda runs down nearly the

full length of one of its sides, and

a high earthen wall faces it on the

Another view of

Ryoan-ji,

showing earthen

wall and

surrounding

trees

opposite side, over which can be

seen some tall trees.

Fifteen stones in five separate groups rise out of the enclosed flat rectangle of ground, surrounded by coarse, white sand, and at the base of each group is a cushion of dark moss. There is a significant space between each rock formation, like a kind of pause in a conversation—a visual silence—and the raked sand between each group isolates them even further, making each one look like an island in a stream. The relative sizes of the rocks and the way they have been rooted in the ground create a sense of perfect harmony and balance.

Some see the equipoise of Zen composure in this display of rocks

and sand. Some see eternity in its
stones. But there is also a legend
suggested by these particular rock
configurations, placing the garden
in the category of idea symbolism.
Another name for this garden is
"The Garden of Crossing Tiger-
Cubs," said to refer to a time when
Confucian ideas from China were
influencing Japan. The rock forma-
tions seen as tigers may symbolize
the Confucian virtue of a just ruler
protecting the country, even from
ferocious beasts. Others see the
scene as a mother tiger carefully
marshalling her cubs to safety
across surging rapids.

Whatever the meaning of Ryoan-ji

—seen as an idea, a mood, a

representation of nature, a pure

spiritual presence, or as visual

music—it expresses through its mul-

tiple meanings the Zen spirit of

sincerity and timelessness. Lying

open and naked under all kinds of

weather, glistening in the rain,

celestial in the snow, Ryoan-ji,

always noble and mysterious, is like

the human heart, something we
never tire of contemplating in all its
changes of mood.

THIS GARDEN

All worries and troubles

have gone from my breast

and I play joyfully

far from the world

For a person of Zen

no limits exist

The blue sky must feel

ashamed to be so small

Muso Soseki (1275–1351)
Japanese Zen master and poet

We've seen, in our mind's eye at
least, various aspects of Zen rock
gardens as they appear in reality.
Going from that imagined reality to
our miniature rock garden is like
looking into a microscope. But
perhaps we may taste something of
the real experience, essentializing

our lives by means of

this miniature replica.

As in so many things in

Zen, the large may be

experienced in the

small, and the cosmic meaning may

be reflected in the

microcosmic gesture.

We may not become

Zen adepts, but any-

thing we do with skill may serve us

well. There is a Zen story of a master

of the tea ceremony who became a

master sword

fighter overnight.

As the story goes,

the tea master

inadvertently insulted a great

samurai swordsman, who immedi-

ately challenged him to a duel the

following morning.

The tea master was terrified.

He ran to the only sword master

he knew and pleaded with him to

train him in one night to become an

able swordsman. But the tea master

was a hopeless student. No matter

how patiently the sword master

tried to teach him, the tea master

remained inept. At last, the sword

master said to him, "Just approach

your swordfight the way you

approach your tea ceremonies,"

and gave up.

The following morning, heavy-

hearted, his fate sealed, the tea

master reluctantly went to his

appointment.

When he faced the

samurai on the

misty hill he shut

his eyes tight,

lifted the heavy

sword above his

head, then concentrated and cen-

tered himself the way he did each

time he performed the tea

ceremony. At that, the samurai

threw down his sword, got down on

his knees, and begged the other

man's forgiveness. "If I had known

you were such a great swordsman,"

he said, "I never would have

challenged you!"

Perhaps we can bring something

of this transference of mastery

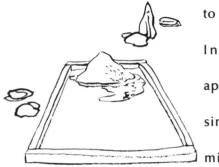

to our Zen garden.

In the inner

appreciation of the

simplicity of this

miniature garden

that we ourselves create, in the abil-

ity to reduce all complexity to a

matter of sand and rocks, graceful

waves etched in the sand contrast-

ing with flinty edges of mica, we

may find

that the

rest of the

universe

has become

simpler for

a moment as well.

We may put any rocks

in the garden we wish—we

might find some that are

eccentric or fiery, saintly,

heroic, or flat like a

boat—we may need a vari-

ety of forms to choose

from when we shake our sand

smooth and set up new dragon-

veins, or relation-

ships, between

them. Various

colors of sand

might also be used

as in real rock

gardens—black to

give an imposing

formality, brown for a subdued and

refined look, and the purest white

to set off the rocks

even more starkly.

Spontaneity and

experimentation are

the key.

The Zen garden is,

after all, a launching

pad—a place to take off

from, and to come back to. Though

the garden seems a perfect setting

for the enlightenment experience,

someone can just as well become

enlightened in heavy traffic, bend-

ing forward to sip fast-food soup, or

while overlooking the city from a

Manhattan highrise.

For after enlightenment, we have

to come back to the same thing we left, for all our remaining days. We might see it with totally new eyes, or, as one Zen master said, perhaps ironically, he was miserable before he was enlightened, and after he became enlightened he was still as miserable as ever.

Someone once came upon Saint Francis hoeing in his garden, and asked him what he would do if he found out that the world would end the following day. Without a pause, Saint Francis replied, "I'd keep hoeing."

The Zen garden is like our lives, which we arrange and put into coherent patterns as best we can, raking swirls in the sand around our

little gritty protuberances of selfhood

in the middle of eternity's ocean-

waves. We continue raking and pick-

ing up leaves, accepting our own

natures, satisfied that we—like grains

of sand—may contain whole worlds.

Perhaps you may notice with new

eyes the sparkling branches outside

your windows, the bending grasses,

trees, and rocks, even your own

thoughts and the thoughts of

others: a wider view. Everything in

its proper place, including you.

Ah, how glorious!
Green leaves, young leaves
Glittering in the sunlight.
Matsuo Basho (1644–1694)
Japanese poet

OTHER GARDENS

Aitken, Robert. *A Zen Wave: Basho's Haiku and Zen.* New York/Tokyo: Weatherhill, 1978.

Engel, David H., Masanobu Kudo, and Kiyoshi Seike. *A Japanese Touch for Your Garden.* Tokyo/New York: Kodansha International Ltd., 1980.

Ferguson, John. *Encyclopedia of Mysticism and Mystery Religions.* New York: Crossroad, 1982.

Fukuda, Kazuhiko. *Japanese Stone Gardens: How to Make and Enjoy Them.* Rutland, VT/Tokyo: Charles E. Tuttle Company, 1970.

Kuck, Loraine. *The World of the Japanese Garden: From Chinese Origins to Modern Landscape Art.* New York: Walker/Weatherhill, 1968.

Legeza, Laszlo and Philip Rawson. *Tao: The Eastern Philosophy of Time and Change.* New York: Avon Publishers, 1973.

Mair, Victor H., translator. *Tao Te Ching: The Classic Book of Integrity and The Way.* New York: Bantam Books, 1990.

Murphy, Wendy B., and the editors of Time-Life Books. *Japanese Gardens.* Alexandria, VA: Time-Life Books, 1979.

Parrinder, Geoffrey, ed. *World Religions: From Ancient History to the Present.*

New York: Facts on File Publications, 1971.

Saito, Katsuo and Sadaji Wada. *Magic of Trees and Stones: Secrets of Japanese Gardening.* New York: Japan Publications Trading Company, 1964.

Soseki, Muso. *Sun at Midnight: Poems and Sermons by Muso Soseki.* Translated by W. S. Merwin and Soiku Shigematsu. San Francisco: North Point Press, 1989.

Sunset Books and Sunset Magazine. *Sunset Ideas for Japanese Gardens.* Menlo Park, CA: Lane Books, 1968.

Suzuki, Daisetz T. *Zen and Japanese Culture.* Bollingen Series LXIV. New York: Princeton University Press, 1959.

Suzuki, Shunryu. *Zen Mind, Beginner's Mind: Informal Talks on Zen Meditation and Practice.* New York/Tokyo: Weatherhill, 1973.

Watts, Alan. *The Way of Zen.* New York: Vintage, 1957.

Winokur, Jon. *Zen to Go.* New York: New American Library, 1989.

The publisher gratefully acknowledges the permission of the

following to reproduce the photographs in this book, on the

pages indicated:

Asian Art Museum of San Francisco, The Avery Brundage Collection: p. 27 (1989.3). Brooklyn Botanic Garden: p. 48 (bottom) [detail] © Estelle Gerard; p. 48 (top) [detail] © Glenn Kopp; p. 49 [detail] © Philip Mullan. The Cleveland Museum of Art: pp. 30, 40, 41, 58. © Nicholas DeVore III Photographers/Aspen: p. 77. © Ric Ergenbright: p. 61. Grant Heilman Photography, Inc.: p. 12 © Runk/Schoenberger. Japan National Tourist Organization: pp. 19, 53, 63 [detail], 86. Japan Airlines Photos by Morris Simoncelli: pp. 24, 67 [detail], 68 [detail], 73, 78, 82. The National Audubon Society Collection/Photo Researchers: p. 54 © Bill Bachman; p. 65 [detail] © Richard Weymouth Brooks; p. 37 © William Carter; p. 84 (bottom) [detail] © Michael P. Gadomski; p. 14 [detail] © F. B. Grunzweig; pp. 11, 28, 38, 56, 71, 88 [detail], 89 © Alexander Lowry; pp. 33, 50 © C. G. Maxwell; p. 10 (top) © Richard Parker; p. 84 (top) [detail] © Leonard Lee Rue IV; p. 10 (bottom) [detail] © John Spragens, Jr.; p. 26 © Alvin E. Staffan; p. 17 © Arthur Tress; p. 84 (middle) [detail] © Myron Wood. © Barbara Thornbury: p. 44. © Michael S. Yamashita: pp. 3, 5, 18, 34, 35, 45, 59, 69, 70, 75, 85, 90. Zis Corporation: pp. 13, 25, 47, 51, 72, 81, 87.